DONALD PEART

Born a Second Time

Spirit with the Spirit

GIBBS PUBLISHING
CONGLOMERATE

Contents

Foreword

All Scriptural references are:

King James Version ("Public Domain"), unless otherwise noted

All bold text and literal parenthetical phrases in the Scripture references are added by the author for clarity. Single quotes are also used in some texts to highlight a literal definition of the original texts.

Dictionary reference includes, but is not limited to, Strong's Concordance, BibleWorks Software, and ISA2 Basic Software

BORN A SECOND TIME

*John 3:4-5: ⁴Nicodemus says unto him, How can a man be born when he is old? can he enter **the second time into his mother's womb**, and be born? ⁵Jesus answered, verily, verily, I say unto you, **except a man be born of water and of the Spirit**, he cannot enter into the kingdom of God.*

Jesus, in his discourse with one of the rulers of the Jews (Nicodemus), made it clear that a person must be born again (or born from above) to **"see"** and to **"enter"** the kingdom of God (John 3:3-5). Nicodemus thought Jesus meant that a person must enter into his mother's womb a second time to be born again. However, Jesus indicated He was/is referring to "spirit" **<u>birth</u>** from "above" and not flesh birth a second time from a mother.

The Lord Jesus then explained to Nicodemus the process of being "born from above," being "born of the Spirit." "Jesus answered, 'amen, amen,' I say unto you, except a man be **born of water and of the Spirit,** he cannot enter into the kingdom of God" (John 3:5). Thus, there is a process of being born from above that involves "water" and "the Spirit." However, before we discuss the Spirit birth, the question must be asked what

1

was in the mind of the Lord Jesus when he said "water?" Was he thinking of water baptism (Acts 10:47)? Was he thinking of the water of his "rhema" word (Ephesians 5:26)? Water baptism does have an application to the saving of the soul relative to washing of the conscience that produces the "answer of a good conscience towards God" (1 Peter 3:20-21).

In addition, Paul also mentioned in Titus 3:5 that there is a "washing of regeneration and renewing of the Holy Spirit." "Washing" implies "water," and thus a "regeneration" (again-birth) is related to "water." In Ephesians 5:26, Paul said there is "washing of water 'in' the 'rhema'"[1] that both sanctifies and cleanses. This same washing of the word (rhema) also "regenerates" in oneness with the Spirit (1 John 5:6).

In conjunction, Peter also said that the "gospel" he "preached" is the "rhema," that causes us to be "born-again" of the incorruptible seed by the word of God. "[23]Being **born again,** not of corruptible seed, but of incorruptible, by the word (logos[2]) of God, which lives and abides 'into the age' …. [25]But the **word (rhema)** of the Lord endures 'into the age.' And this is the word (rhema) which by the **gospel is preache**d unto you" (1 Peter 1:23; 25). The gospel being preached by a living voice (rhema) is the catalyst for being "being born again." Hence, being born from above of "water" in oneness with the Spirit, may speak of the being born again of water of the word of God, preaching Jesus is the Christ, the Son of the living God.

---

[1] Rhema can be defined as words spoken from a living voice.

[2] One of the definitions of "logos" indicates that "logos" consists both "rhema" [living voice (i.e., a verb, adjective)] and onoma [name(i.e., a subject)].

With that said, Jesus also said a man must be "**born** of water **and of the Spirit**" (John 3:5). Thus, there is "spirit" birth (above-birth) being born again of "the Spirit" (**spirit with the Spirit**). This rebirthing of our human spirit can only be performed by the Spirit of Truth when the rebirthing occurs. The Spirit, then, bears witness with our spirits that we are born of him (Romans 8:16).

That is, Jesus said, "⁷Marvel not that I said unto you, you must be born again. ⁸The 'Spirit breathes' where it 'wills,' and **you hear the sound** thereof, but cannot 'perceive' where it comes, and where it goes: **so is every one that is born 'out of' the Spirit**" (John 3:7-8). Jesus tells us that as we cannot perceive the way of the Spirit, yet we can hear it, so is everyone that is born of the Spirit. Saying it another way, the internal rebirthing of the spirit of a believer can be witnessed by the sound (tone, voice) of the Spirit (or the sound, tone, and voice of our spirit). However, we cannot tell how the birthing occurs because it is an internal work in the inner man by the Holy Spirit. Ecclesiastes 11:5 says that, as we cannot tell how the bones of a baby grow in the womb and the ways of the Spirit, so we cannot know the works of God. The mystery of the rebirthing of our spirit is only known by the living God. However, the Spirit does confirm to us internally and individually that we are born of Him upon belief that Jesus is the Christ (I John 5:1)!

*Romans 8:14-16: ¹⁴For as many as are led by the Spirit of God, they are the **sons** of God. ¹⁵For you have not received **the spirit** of 'slavery' again to fear; but you have received the Spirit of 'son-placing,' whereby we cry, Abba, Father. ¹⁶**The Spirit itself bears witness with our spirit**, that we are the **children** of God.*

Pursuant to reading Paul's writing above, it can be seen that we are called "sons of God," mature sons and sons who are heirs (Romans 8:14). However, when he spoke of the Holy Spirit "bearing witness with our spirits" confirming we are God's children, he uses a Greek word "teknon." "Teknon" speaks more to the **"birthing"** process of the "spirits" of God's offspring rather than the spirits of His "mature" sons and daughters.

*Romans 8:16: The Spirit itself bears witness with our spirit, that we are the **children** (**teknon**) of God.*

The Greek word for "children" is "teknon," which is from "tiko" which means **"to give birth,"** to produce (Matthew 1:21; 2:2; Luke 2:6). Thus, the emphasis of the Spirit bearing witness with our spirits is related to our spirits being His "children" "born of the Spirit." That is, as Elizabeth physically birthed John the Baptist in Luke 1:57, so likewise our spirits are birthed from above, by the Holy Spirit, which is a real rebirth of the spirits of us who believe that Jesus is the Christ.

In addition, as Jesus indicated in John 3:8, we cannot tell when, how, or where the Spirit rebirths our spirits. So Paul has stated that it is the Spirit who can confirm to us that we are His offspring. Or it is the Spirit who confirms we are given birth by the Spirit in our spirits. The phrase "bear witness" is a compound Greek word consisting of sun (together) and" martureó" (witness). One of the definitions of "martureo" means to assert what one has seen and heard to be true (being a witness).

Thus, it is only the Holy Spirit who can assert that we are born a second time because He is the one who born-again our spirits. The Holy Spirit is the one who first **saw** the rebirth, because He performed the birthing. He is the one who first **heard** the "sound"[3] of the spirit rebirth, because He performed the birthing; and the "Spirit is Truth." Thus, as the Lord Jesus affirmed, we must be born a second time in our spirits, by the Holy Spirit washing us in regeneration and the renewal (birthing) of the Holy Spirit. All who desire to "enter" the kingdom of God must be born from above. All who desire to "see" the kingdom of God must be born from above. Our spirits must be born from above a second time through the Spirit of the living God.

With all that said, this is the pragmatic way to be born a second time from above. The beloved apostle John says, "Whoever **believes that Jesus is the Christ** is **born** of God ..." (1 John 5:1). As we just read, to be born **"out of"** God, being born a second time, happens for those who **believe** that **Jesus** is **the Christ.**" The apostle Paul says it this way: "[9]that if you confess with your **mouth the Lord Jesus** and **believe in your heart** that God has **raised Him** from the dead, **you will be saved.** [10]For with the heart one believes unto righteousness, and with the mouth confession is made unto salvation" (Romans 10:9-10).

---

[3] As a baby usually cries at birth, so our spirit "cry abba Father" (Romans 8:15).

WE ARE SPIRIT

*John 3:6: That which is born of the flesh is flesh; and **that which is born of the Spirit is spirit.***

Once we (our spirits) are born a second time, born from above, born of the Holy Spirit, we are now considered "spirit." And each born-again believer is to function as "spirit." Jesus made it clear, **"that which is born of the Spirit is spirit."** Paul also taught a similar principle. Using the example of a male and female copulation to exemplify the oneness of flesh, he equated this principle to believers' oneness of spirit with our Lord Jesus Christ. This oneness of spirit occurs once we are joined to our Lord Jesus by the Holy Spirit.

*1 Corinthians 6:16-17: [16]What? know you not that he which is joined to a harlot is one body? For **two, says he, shall be one flesh.** [17]But he that is **joined** unto the Lord is **one spirit.***

Through the joining of the Holy Spirit with our spirits, we become "one spirit" with the Lord Jesus. Hence, as our Lord Jesus has said, "that which is born of the Spirit is spirit." You are spirit, with a soul which is housed in a body. With that said, the Greek word used for "joined" is from a Greek root transliterated to our English word "glue." In addition, this Greek word "kalloa," in classical Greek, is used of the healing of a cut of which the laceration is now healed (united again). We are one spirit with our Lord's Spirit by being joined to His Spirit, glued as "one." This oneness occurs when we are filled with the Holy Spirit, or when we have received the Holy Spirit. This is a separate experience from being born of the Holy Spirit. Thus, being "one spirit" with the Lord, we are to function in the excellent quality of Spirit, and not in the sinful tendency of the flesh nature.

With that said, it is the spirit that keeps our bodies alive. "The body without the spirit is dead" (James 2:26). The Spirit gives life or is life producing (John 6:63). The soul cannot produce life. God also communicates with us with His Spirit to our spirits (Romans 8:16). "God is Spirit (John 4:24)! God is "the Father of the spirits" of all flesh (Hebrews 12:9, Numbers 16:22,; 27:16). And we are made in His image spirit, soul, and body.

JESUS AS SPIRIT

*John 3:6: That which is born of the flesh is flesh; and **that which is born of the Spirit is spirit.***

*Matthew 1:18; 20-21: [18]Now the **birth** of Jesus Christ was on this wise: when as his mother Mary was espoused to Joseph, before they came together, **she was found with child of the Holy Ghost** .... [20]But while [Joseph] thought on these things, behold, the angel of the Lord appeared unto him in a dream, saying, Joseph, you son of David, fear not to take unto you Mary your wife: **for that which is conceived in her is of the Holy Ghost**. [21]And she shall bring forth a son, and you shall call his name JESUS: for he shall save his people from their sins.*

As believers are born again in spirit with the Holy Spirit, and thus, considered "spirit," so likewise, our Lord Jesus was born "spirit" and therefore also considered as "spirit." As indicated above, "now **the birth** of Jesus Christ was on this wise: ... his mother ... [Mary] was found with **child of the Holy Spirit**." Thus, as Jesus said, "**that which is born of the Spirit is spirit**."

It follows that Jesus also functioned as "spirit" when he walked the earth in the flesh as Christ, the Son of God. When he was on his way to resurrect Lazarus, he "groaned in his spirit." This occurred when he saw the people weeping over Lazarus' death. This "groaning in spirit" hints that resurrection power flows from God's Spirit through our spirits. Here is the reference: "Therefore, when Jesus saw her weeping, and the Jews who came with her weeping, He **groaned in the spirit** and was troubled" (John 11:33). In addition when Jesus finally arrived at the tomb to perform the resurrection it is also written: "Then Jesus, again **groaning in Himself** ... (John 11:38-39). The Greek word translated as "groaned" or "groaning" properly means to snort like an angry horse. Thus, questions can be asked: Was Jesus angry at their unbelief?

Was Jesus angry at Death? Was Jesus angry that they were sorrowful and weeping, not realizing Jesus, "the resurrection" personified, was in their midst? Was his "groaning" in the Spirit to help their weaknesses (Romans 8:26). We may not know for sure, but one thing we know, in the process leading up to Jesus resurrecting Lazarus, His "spirit" was involved! Because, though he lived in a body, He is considered Spirit because he was born of the Holy Spirit.

With that said, another spirit function of Jesus was seen during His prayer in the garden just before His betrayal and crucifixion. During His strenuous prayer in the garden, Jesus had experiences in all three parts of Himself (His soul, His flesh and His Spirit, Matthew 24:38; 24: 41). With respect to Jesus "Spirit" functions, it was the "before-feelings" of His Spirit that encouraged him to pray through the sorrowfulness of His soul.

Matthew 24:38; 40-41: ³⁸*Then says he unto them, my soul is*

9

*exceeding sorrowful, even unto death: tarry you here, and watch with me .... ⁴⁰And he comes unto the disciples, and finds them asleep, and says unto Peter, what, could you not watch with me one hour? ⁴¹Watch and pray, that you enter not into temptation: **the spirit** indeed is **willing** (**lit., feels-before**), but the flesh is weak.*

The soul can be overwhelmed with sorrow, the flesh is weak; however, the spirit of a person (especially the spirit of a born-again believer) can "feel" things that are to happen beforehand." In the middle of Jesus "feeling-before" hand emotions related to the death He was about to experience (the emotions of the "sorrow" of the soul and feeling the "weakness" of the flesh), **Jesus' spirit was "willing"** to continue to pray until both flesh (body) and soul submitted to the will of God.

In Jesus' first of three times praying concerning Him drinking the cup of the suffering of the cross, Jesus asked, "My Father, if it be possible, let this cup pass from me" (see Matthew 26:39). However, in his last of the three times of prayer in the garden, praying in conjunction with the spirit being able to feel the upcoming suffering, he submitted to the will of the heavenly Father.

Jesus said, "⁴¹Watch and pray, that you enter not into temptation: **the spir**it indeed '**before-feels**,' but the flesh is weak. ⁴²He went away again the second time, and prayed, saying, O my Father, if this cup may not pass away from me, except I drink it, **your will be done ....** ⁴⁴And he left them, and went away again, and prayed the third time, saying the same words" (Matthew 24:41-42; 44). Thus, we see that Jesus, though he was in a physical body, also functioned as "Spirit" with His Spirit.

HAVING THE SPIRIT

Romans 8:9: But you are not in the flesh, but in the Spirit, if so be that the Spirit of God dwells in you. **Now if any man have not the Spirit of Christ, he is none of his.**

Paul stated that if anyone does **"not have"** the Spirit of Christ, that person is not of Christ. Thus, the question must be asked is "The Spirit of Christ," we are supposed to "have" our spirit that is of Christ? Or is "the Spirit of Christ" we are supposed to "have" the Spirit of Christ, Himself, in us, after being filled or baptized with the Holy Spirit? The answer is yes to both questions. The phrase "the Spirit of Christ" is used only twice in the scriptures, the second time by the Apostle Peter. Peter stated that the prophets of God, identified in the Old Testament, had "the Spirit of Christ in them" who testified beforehand of the salvation related to the suffering of Christ.

1 Peter 1:9-11: ⁹Receiving the end of your faith, even the salvation of your souls. ¹⁰Of which salvation the prophets have inquired and searched diligently, who prophesied of the grace that should come unto you: ¹¹Searching what, or what manner of time **the Spirit of Christ, which was in them** *did signify, when it testified beforehand the sufferings of Christ, and the glory that should follow.*

The reference above makes it clear that the Spirit of Christ was **"in"** the prophets who spoke. That is, it was "Christ, Himself, "in them by His Holy Spirit. Thus, Paul's statement saying, "if any man have not the Spirit of Christ, he is none of his," relates to the Spirit of Christ in us as a separate experience from being born of the Spirit. This is confirmed in the pattern Son, Jesus, the Christ. He was first conceived by the Holy Spirit in Mary, and he was filled with the same Spirit in a separate experience around age thirty (30). Here are the proofs of the two (2) separate experiences of being born of the Spirit and having the Spirit:

Jesus was Conceived of the Holy Spirit

*Matthew 1:18; 20-21: [18]Now the **birth** of Jesus Christ was on this wise: when as his mother Mary was espoused to Joseph, before they came together, **she was found with child of the Holy Ghost** .... [20]But while [Joseph] thought on these things, behold, the angel of the Lord appeared unto him in a dream, saying, Joseph, you son of David, fear not to take unto you Mary your wife: **for that which is conceived in her is of the Holy Ghost.** [21]And she shall bring forth a son, and you shall call his name JESUS: for he shall save his people from their sins.*

From the verses above, we see that Jesus was indeed conceived of the Holy Spirit. That is, the Holy Spirit produced Jesus in the womb of Mary, just as it is the Holy Spirit who "procreates" our spirits again. Thus, as Jesus was born of the Spirit, we are also birth of the Spirit. As we will see in a moment, the "birthing" process is also defined a "**Christ** being formed **in** us"

Jesus was Filled with the Holy Spirit

Luke 3:21-23;4:1: *²¹Now when all the people were baptized, it came to pass, that Jesus also being baptized, and praying, the heaven was opened, ²²And the Holy Spirit descended in a bodily shape like a dove upon him, and a voice came from heaven, which said, You are my beloved Son; in You I am well pleased. ²³And Jesus himself began to be about thirty years of age .... ⁴:¹And **Jesus being full of the Holy Spirit** returned from Jordan, and was led by the Spirit into the wilderness*

In the references above, we see that Jesus was indeed filled with the Holy Spirit as a separate experience from being procreated by the same Holy Spirit. This baptism of the Spirit occurred when Jesus was thirty (30). The same is true for all who are born of the Holy Spirit a second time, we must also be filled or baptized with the Holy Spirit in a separate experience.

Once we are filled with the Spirit, or baptized with the Spirit, we are considered as "having the Spirit of Christ" in us. "But you are not in the flesh, but in the Spirit, if so be that **the Spirit of God dwells in you.** Now if any man **have not the Spirit of Christ**, he is none of his" (Romans 8:9).

It follows that "whosoever believes that Jesus is the Christ is **born out of God**" (1 John 5:1). The phrase "born out of God" references our spirit being born again. We have a spirit born of Christ! We are Christ's! In addition, whosoever receives the Holy Spirit baptism "has" the Spirit and now belongs to Christ, in the sense of also being "in Christ." Being "in Christ" is synonymous with being baptized into the Body of Christ, which has spiritual benefits (compare 1 Corinthians 12, Galatians 4, Galatians 5, Romans 8, etc.). With that said, here is another reference that shows we must receive the Spirit after we believe as a separate experience.

Acts 19:1-7: ¹And it came to pass, that, while Apollos was at Corinth, Paul having passed through the upper coasts came to Ephesus: and finding certain disciples, ²He said unto them, **Have you received the Holy Spirit since ye believed?** *And they said unto him, we have not so much as heard whether there be any Holy Spirit. ³And he said unto them, unto what then were you baptized? And they said, unto John's baptism. ⁴Then said Paul, John verily baptized with the baptism of repentance, saying unto the people, that they should believe on him which should come after him, that is, on Christ Jesus. ⁵When they heard this, they were baptized in the name of the Lord Jesus. ⁶And when Paul had laid his hands upon them,* **the Holy Spirit came on them;** *and they spoke with tongues, and prophesied. ⁷And all the men were about twelve.*

The twelve disciples at Ephesus were born again by the Holy Spirit because they "believed" that Jesus is the Christ (1 John 5:1, John 3). In addition, they were also filled with the Holy Spirit, as a separate experience. This second experience of being filled with the Holy Spirit caused them to "have the Spirit of Christ," and thus, they are also now "in Christ." Since a Spirit-filled believer is now in Christ, the believer is no longer in the flesh but "in the Spirit." Also, in this record of some disciples being born of the Spirit by believing, and then being filled with the Spirit, the "sound," "tone," or "voice" confirming Spirit function was witnessed by them speaking in tongues and prophesying.

Christ Formed in Us by Birthing

*Galatians 4:19: My little children, of whom I travail in **birth again** until **Christ be formed in** you.*

In this verse, we see that "Christ" is **"in"** us through the birthing process. Paul had to go through the **"pain"** of the **"birthing"** process **"again"** for the Church at Galatia. (This rebirthing of the Church a Galatia had to occur because they reverted to their flesh nature.) The "parturition" process is part of how Christ is "formed" in us. Yes, Christ is **formed** **"in"** us through the pain of birth. Therefore, the Spirit of Christ **in us** is both through the birthing process (the pain of being formed) and through the separate experience of being filled with the Spirit of Christ. Paul made this understanding of Christ being "in" us through the birthing process clear in Galatians chapter four verse twenty-nine. Paul spoke of them experiencing persecution for being "**born** … according to **the Spirit;" Paul helping in the process through birth pains on their behalf.**

Thus, when Paul said, "Now if any man have not the Spirit of Christ, **he is none of his,**" it has to be **also** understood from the perspective of Christ being in us through the birthing process. This same apostle (Paul) also said it is "because we are sons" (legitimately birthed) we are then given the "Spirit of His Son," the filling of the Spirit of the Lord Jesus (Galatians 4:6). That is, we are His, "because" we are "sons," first, through "birth" ("Christ being **formed in** us") before we are subsequently filled, much more of Christ in us!

In fact, the literal definition of the phrase "if so be," in Romans chapter eight verse nine, is literally translated as "if much." "But you are not in the flesh, but in the Spirit, **'if much'** Spirit of God dwells in you ...." That is, we are graced to have the Spirit of Christ in us through the pain of birthing, and we are also graced to have "much" more of the Spirit of Christ in us when we are filled with the Holy Spirit.

Saying it another way, **we are the heavenly Father's "sons,"** because Christ is formed **in us** through **faith** with the **pain of birthing** (Galatians 3:25; 4:6; 4:19). This is understood by reading Galatians chapters three and four. Since we are "sons" before being filled, we are His (the heavenly Father's). Therefore, this birthing of "Christ being formed in us" (Christ is the Spirit) precedes being filled by the same Spirit in a separate experience. As it is written, "And **because** you are **sons,** God has sent forth the Spirit of His Son **into** your hearts, crying Abba, Father" (Galatians 4:6).

Again, the fact that we are "sons" (Christ being formed in us), before He sends His Spirit to be "into" us, means that we are His (we have Christ's Spirit). This is before the subsequent filing of the Spirit. The filling of the Spirit is given to "bear witness" that we are indeed God's offspring! We are His! "The Spirit bears witness with our spirits that we are the children of God" (Romans 8:16).

HOW TO RECEIVE THE SPIRIT

Luke 11:9-13: *⁹And I say unto you, Ask, and it shall be given you; seek, and you shall find; knock, and it shall be opened unto you.* *¹⁰For everyone that asks receives; and he that seeks finds; and to him that knocks it shall be opened.* *¹¹If a son shall ask bread of any of you that is a father, will he give him a stone? or if he ask a fish, will he for a fish give him a serpent?* *¹²Or if he shall ask an egg, will he offer him a scorpion?* *¹³If you then, being evil, know how to give good gifts unto your children:* **how much more shall your heavenly Father give the Holy Spirit to them that ask him?**

Since there is an apparent requirement to be filled with the Holy Spirit, it is appropriate that I show some of the documented ways believers received the Holy Spirit. And be it known that upon being baptized in the Holy Spirit, they are now considered as "**having** the Spirit of Christ."

Firstly, in the reference above, Jesus made it clear that the heavenly father will never give us anything evil "if" and "when" we ask for the Holy Spirit. He contrasted the generosity of evil fathers on the earth who would not give something opposite to what their sons and daughters asked for, compared to the heavenly Father, who will give the Holy Spirit to those who ask for the Spirit. As Jesus said, no father of a son or daughter would give him/her a stone if either asked for bread. No father of a son or daughter will give him/her a serpent if either asks for a fish. No father of a son or daughter will give him/her a scorpion if either asks for an egg. **"How much more shall your heavenly Father give the Holy Spirit to them that ask him?"**

Filled with the Spirit Without Man's Hands

With that said, a person can be filled with the Spirit by asking the heavenly Father personally without any other human involved. This happened in Acts chapter two when the first one hundred twenty (120) received the Holy Spirit. God sovereignly poured out His Holy Spirit on them and in them.

> *"1. And when the day of Pentecost was fully come, they were all with one accord in one place. 2. And suddenly there came a sound from heaven as of a rushing mighty wind, and it filled all the house where they were sitting. 3. And there appeared unto them* ***'distributed'*** *tongues like as of fire, and it sat upon each of them. 4. And they were all filled with the Holy* ***'Spirit,'*** **and began to speak with other tongues, as the Spirit gave them utterance"** *(Acts 2:1-4).*

Filled with the Spirit Through Preaching

Another way to be filled with the Spirit is by hearing the preaching of the gospel of Jesus Christ. The apostle Peter preached to Cornelius, the Centurian and his household; and as Peter preached, Cornelius and his household were filled or baptized with the Holy Spirit. Thus, when a true man of God preaches the gospel of Jesus, God can sovereignly come upon them and in them with the Holy Spirit.

> ⁴²*And [Jesus] commanded us to preach unto the people, and to testify that it is [Jesus] which was ordained of God to be the Judge of 'living' and dead.* ⁴³*To him give all the prophets witness, that through his name whosoever believeth in him shall receive remission of sins.* ⁴⁴**While Peter yet spoke these words, the Holy 'Spirit' fell on all them** *which heard the word.* ⁴⁵*And they of the circumcision which believed were astonished, as many as came with Peter, because that **on the Gentiles also was poured out the gift of the Holy 'Spirit.'*** ⁴⁶*For they heard them speak with tongues, and magnify God (Acts 10:42-46).*

Filled with the Spirit by Laying on of Hands

Another way to receive the gift of the Holy Spirit is by apostles and prophets laying their hands upon a believer. This laying on of the hands by foundation ministries was demonstrated by apostles Peter and John in Acts chapter eight. And demonstrated by Apostle Paul in Acts chapter nineteen. It is also worth noting that this same application is also true today.

> ¹⁴*Now when the apostles which were at Jerusalem heard that Samaria had received the word of God, they sent unto them Peter and John:* ¹⁵*Who, when they were come down, prayed for them, that they might receive the Holy 'Spirit:'*

[16](For as yet he was fallen upon none of them: only they were baptized in the name of the Lord Jesus.) [17]***Then laid they their hands on them, and they received the Holy 'Spirit''*** *(Acts 8:14-17).*

Thus, a believer, today, can ask for the Holy Spirit in private, and the Lord will fill them with His Spirit. A person can hear a powerful message about Jesus being preached and be filled. Or a person can receive the baptism of the Holy Spirit by godly ministers laying hands on that person to receive the Holy Spirit.

Manifestations of the Holy Spirit

We have been erroneously taught that the only sign that a person is filled with the Spirit is the evidence of speaking with other tongues. Though it does appear that speaking in tongues is the prevalent manifestation that a person is filled. The apostle Paul made it clear that the evidence of being filled is diverse. The manifestations of being filled include, but are not limited to, the following: the apostle Paul listed in 1 Corinthians 12:5-11:

*[4]Now there are diversities of gifts, but **the same Spirit.** [5]And there are differences of administrations, but **the same Lord.** [6]And there are diversities of operations, but it is **the same God** which worketh all in all. [7]But **the manifestation of the Spiri**t is given to every man to profit withal. [8]For to one is given **by the Spirit the word of wisdom;** to another the word of knowledge **by the same Spirit;** [9]To another **faith by the same Spirit;** to another **the gifts of healing by the same Spirit;** [10]To another the **working of miracles (lit., powers);** to another **prophecy;***

20

> *to another **discerning of spirits;** to another **divers kinds of tongues;** to another the **interpretation of tongues:*** **¹¹But all these worketh that one and the selfsame Spirit, dividing to every man severally as he will.**

It is the "same Spirit" that manifests these nine gifts of the Spirit. Yes, there are at least twenty-two gifts of the Spirit, nine of which are listed above as manifestations of the Spirit that confirm a believer has the Holy Spirit in them. Paul also made it clear that "not all speak with tongues," "not all have the gifts of healing" (see Greek text for 1 Corinthians 12:29-30). Thus, we don't have the right to discourage someone by telling them they are not filled if they don't speak with other tongues.

The signs that the Holy Spirit is in a person are confirmed to an individual by the manifestation that God, the Spirit, chooses. Paul said in 1 Corinthians 12:29-30, as read in all the original Greek texts, "²⁹ 'Not' all are apostles! 'Not' all are prophets! 'Not' all are teachers! 'Not' all are miracles. ³⁰'Not' all have the gifts of healing! **'Not' all speak with tongues!** 'Not' all interpret!"

Paul made it clear that "not all speak with tongues;" hence, tongues is only one (1) of the manifestations of the Holy Spirit in a believer's life. The Lord Jesus declared that the original one hundred-twenty (120) disciples would experience to confirm that they are filled was "power" or "miracle."

The work of power or miracles is only one (1) of the manifestations of the Holy Spirit Paul also listed (1 Corinthians 12:10; 12:28). The Lord Jesus said, "But you shall receive power when

the Holy Spirit has come upon you …." (Acts 1:8). Yes in addition to "power" the original one hundred-twenty received, they did also speak with tongues. However, the declaration that "power" in the life of a believer is one (1) of the signs of being filled with the Spirit and should not be taken away by any.

HOW TO WALK IN SPIRIT

1 Corinthians 14:14-15: [14]For if I pray in an unknown tongue, **my spirit prays,** *but my understanding is unfruitful. [15]What is it then? I* **will pray with the spirit,** *and I will pray with the understanding also: I will* **sing with the spirit***, and I will sing with the understanding also.*

In 1 Corinthians chapter twelve, Paul laid out most of the twenty-two gifts of the Spirit by first listing nine of the more prevalent gifts of the Spirit, which he also labels as "spiritual" (1 Corinthians 12:1). Among these gifts of the Spirit is speaking in tongues. Thus, speaking in tongues and all the other spiritual gifts Paul, Peter, and others listed are a function of "spirit." So, how do we walk in the Spirit functioning in all of the gifts and fruits of the Spirit? I will use a statement by Paul to show the simplicity of walking in the Spirit.

Paul said whenever he prays or speaks in an unknown tongue, "his spirit" is praying or speaking. Thus, speaking in tongues is a "spirit function." It follows that all the gifts and the fruit(s) of the Spirit are a spirit function. That is, as I can easily and by choice (because it is a gift from the Spirit) speak in tongues, which is a spirit function;" so likewise, I can function in all of the manifestations of the spiritual gifts of the Holy Spirit. As I can easily speak in tongues or pray in tongues, and it is a spirit function; so likewise, when I pray for healing using the gift of healing, it is a spirit function through the Holy Spirit. I don't have to conjure up any emotions or over-extended prayer to make it look like I am spiritual or functioning in spirit. All I need to do is simply believe, lay hands, and pray, all of which is a spirit function, doing this as easily as when I pray in tongues, which is praying with my spirit.

Another example is whenever the Holy Spirit in you begins to manifest the "discerning of spirits (discerning God's Spirit, man's spirit, angels' spirits), know that it is a spirit function. Why? Because distinguishing various spirits is a gift of the Holy Spirit and a manifestation of walking in the Spirit of God through your spirit. So, in walking in the spirit, please don't make it hard or be overly spiritual by manufacturing bodily gestures, making weird sounds, and so on to function in the Spirit. Walking in the Holy Spirit in oneness with your spirit is to be as natural as walking.

With all that said, being (existing) in the Spirit, walking with the Spirit (the Spirit is instrumental), and walking to the Spirit (the Spirit is the location) happen when the Holy Spirit personally makes His "home" in us. For, "you are not in the flesh, but **in the Spirit,** if so be that **the Spirit of God 'homes'** in you … (Romans 8:9).

MATURED SPIRIT

Hebrews 12:22-23: ²²*But you are come unto mount Sion, and unto the city of the living God, the heavenly Jerusalem, and to an innumerable company of angels,* ²³*To the general assembly and church of the 'firstborns,' which are written in heaven, and to God the Judge of all, and to* **the spirits of just men made 'mature.'**

When we are born of the Spirit, our spirit is made new, young, immature, and must be matured by God. This is exemplified by John the Baptist. It is said that after John's birth, he "**grew** and waxed strong **in spirit**"(Luke 1:80). Yes, the spirit of John the Baptist had to **grow** into maturity. He also had to be governed to function with his spirit. The same is true for all believers, our spirits must grow into maturity.

That is, just as our body matures from a baby into adulthood, so likewise our born-again spirits must mature from being immature into maturity. Yet, there are many people who have mature bodies; however, their internal spirits are immature, and they also have diminutive (underdeveloped) souls. That is, people may have a mature body, but act as a child in spirit (childish "in part" disposition, incomplete, "in part," logic, and underdeveloped speech) and a diminutive soul (seeing oneself as small and insignificant).

In Hebrews 12:23 cited above, we read that the "spirits of just men were made mature." This statement gives insight related to the maturing of the spirit. One, the maturing of spirits is linked to being "just." Secondly, the maturity of spirits is a result that God produces. Their spirits were made mature (passive voice in the Greek) by God.

That is, God is the one who acted upon their spirits to mature them due to them being "just."[4] As it is the Holy Spirit that births our spirits again, so likewise it is the Spirit of the living God who also matures our spirits. With that said, and without getting into all the details, a person with a mature spirit willingly subjects his/her spirit to the living God. The living God is both Lord and God of his/her spirit.

*Revelation 22:6, BSB: Then the angel said to me, "These words are faithful and true. **The Lord, the God of the spirits of the prophets**, has sent His angel to show His servants what must soon take place."*

*1 Corinthians 14:29-32, BSB: [29]Two or three prophets should speak, and the others should weigh carefully what is said. [30]**And if a revelation comes to someone who is seated, the first speaker should stop.** [31]For you can all prophesy in turn so that everyone may be instructed and encouraged. [32]**The spirits of prophets are subject to prophets.***

---

[4] "Just" can be defined as rightly aligned to and practicing customs considered appropriate (in the case of a believer, we are to align to God's customs). In the New Testament, the "just" live by faith. It is through faith in the living God we are justified (Romans 1:17, Galatians 3:11, Hebrews 10:38).

In 1 Corinthians 14:30 and 14:32, we see that a prophet's spirit is subject to himself. The same is true for a prophetess. The prophet is able to control his prophetic revelation or speech because the prophet's spirit is subject to him. Therefore, a prophet or prophetess can also choose to rightfully submit his/her spirit to the "Lord God."

Thus, a mature spirit allows Jesus' lordship of their spirit and allows the living God to place his/her spirit where God so wills it to be. Because the Greek word for Lord (Kyrios) means "a person exercising absolute ownership rights," The Greek word for God (Theos) means the Placer. Thus, a mature spirit is subjected to the ownership rights and placing rights of the living God. That is, the Lord God is sovereign over our spirits, and sends the spirit of His prophets "subjected" to Him where He wills.

This maturity of spirit principle was demonstrated by Paul (among others like the beloved apostle John exemplified in Revelation 4:1-2 and Revelation 1:10); Paul's experiences are documented in two locations in the Scriptures of Truth. God was able to place Paul's spirit at locations where Paul was not present in body. In 1 Corinthians 5:3-4, we read that although Paul was "absent in body" at the Corinthians Church, he was present in "spirit."

Paul also relayed similar mature work of the spirits of just men in Colossians 2:1-5. Paul again said, "For **though I be absent in the flesh, yet am I with you in the spirit,** joying and beholding your order, and the steadfastness of your faith in Christ." This same principle of the spirits of just men who were made mature being "placed" by God is also understood in the book of Revelation. In the book of Revelation, a student of the living God will discover that some of the angels were indeed prophets and apostles.

SPIRIT SOUND

*Romans 8:16: The Spirit itself **bears witness with our spirit**, that we are the children of God.*

The Spirit of God communicates (bears witness) with our spirits. The Spirit of God affirms to our spirits what He has seen and heard and communicates that to our spirits. Our Lord Jesus declared in John 3:8 that the Spirit has a "sound," or "voice," or "tone."

*John 3:8: The 'Spirit breathes' where it 'wills,' and **you hear the sound** thereof, but cannot 'perceive' where it comes, and where it goes: **so is every one that is born 'out of' the Spirit**.*

Every spirit (God's, humans,' angels') has a "sound." Every believer, born of the Spirit, has a sound or voice or tone that confesses the Lord Jesus. The word "sound" used in the text above and other places is translated from the Greek word "phóné." This word " phóné" is transliterated to English as "phone," over which we communicate with people near and far. "Phóné" also means voice, tone, language, and dialect. Thus, we see that every spirit has a sound, voice, and tone. Therefore, it is plausible for the Holy Spirit to communicate with our spirits.

The Spirit does have a voice, tone, and sound. The Spirit of God speaks, and so do our spirits.

1 Timothy 4:1a says, "Now **the Spirit speaks** expressly ...." This verse is referencing the Spirit of the living God that speaks. Therefore, our spirits can hear the speech, voice, tone, and sound of the Holy Spirit. In addition, the beloved apostle John also taught that spirits speak. In one of his writings to the elect saints, John made it very clear that many false prophets' spirits went out into the world to deceive as many as they could.

In his discourse, the beloved apostle John made it clear that "spirits ... confesses," where the Greek word translated as "confess" means "to say the same thing." In John's example, the spirits of the false prophets were <u>**not**</u> "saying the same thing" as their mouths were saying. There is a difference between the voice of the spirit born from above, as opposed to the voice of the soul spoken through one's mouth. The voice of the spirit is generally pleasant to the senses (mild). The voice of the soul is usually unpleasant to the senses (bitter).

*1 John 4:1-2: ¹Beloved, believe not every spirit, but try the spirits whether they are of God: because many false prophets are gone out into the world. ²Hereby know you the Spirit of God: Every **spirit that confesses** that Jesus Christ is come in the flesh is of God: ³And every spirit that confesses **not** that Jesus Christ is come in the flesh is not of God: and **this is that 'of-the' antichrist**, whereof ye have heard that it should come; and even now already is it in the world.*

The previous references make it clear that the beloved apostle John taught that "spirits" have speech. In the case of true prophets, their **spirit must "say the same thing"** that their mouth is saying that Jesus has come in the flesh. In the case of false prophets, their mouths may say that Jesus came in the flesh; however, their spirit confesses the opposite or differently (i.e., no internal mildness). They are false because outwardly they look like sheep (their mouths deceptively pretend to be of Jesus Christ by their sayings); however, inwardly, their spirit's voice, tone, sound expose them as false (rapacious attitudes). False prophets' spirits really do not confess ("say the same thing") in their spirits that Jesus confessed in His Spirit when Jesus came in the flesh. Jesus' Spirit always confessed the love of the heavenly Father for humanity. That is, Jesus' Spirit confessed God's kindness and long suffering towards humanity.

Thus, it is very apparent that false prophets' spirits have a voice, a sound, a tone, a speech, or a signal that is Antichrist's. Their spirits in reality say things that are against Christ. Yes, the truth still holds that spirits have a voice, a sound, a tone, either of the living God or of other voices not of God. God does indeed speak to his born-again believers by His Holy Spirit to our spirits. Hence, we must study God and allow Him to develop our spirits to hear His Spirit clearly.

SPIRIT UNDERSTANDING

Colossians 1:7-9: *[7]As you also learned of Epaphras our dear fellow-servant, who is for you a faithful minister of Christ; [8]Who also declared unto us your love in the Spirit. [9]For this cause we also, since the day we heard it, do not cease to pray for you, and to desire that you might be filled with the knowledge of his will in all wisdom and **spiritual understanding**.*

Upon Paul being informed of the "love in the Spirit" of the saints at Colosse, he did not cease to pray that they might be filled with "all … **spiritual understanding**." This "spiritual understanding" comes from the Holy Spirit. It is Spirit understanding and not fleshly, earthy, or worldly understanding.

The definition for "spiritual" means "of the spirit," "things of the spirit," hence "spiritual." In addition, "understanding" is a Greek compound word, "sunesis" [together(sun)-send or put (hiemi)]. We get our English word "synthesis" from this Greek word. Synthesis means to combine into a comprehensive whole, to combine into a logical whole. Hence, there is the capacity to understand things of the Spirit, spiritual things, comprehensively, logically, not just in part, but as a "whole." Again, according to Paul, this Holy Spirit understanding, spiritual understanding, can only be given to those who "love in the Spirit." With that said, what are **some** of the ways that the Spirit of God gives us understanding?

1. The Spirit of God gives us understanding by "revelation," "unveiling" his wisdom (clarity) to us (1 Corinthians 2:10).

- Revelation knowledge about the mystery of Jesus and His Church that only comes from the Spirit (Ephesians 3:5-6).
- For example, by revelation of the Spirit, it was always God's plan to have a Church consisting of Jews and Gentiles. The Gentile believers are not an afterthought (Ephesians 1, Ephesians 3).

2. The Spirit of God gives us his "deep things" by "inquiry" searches (1 Corinthians 2:10).

- There are some things for our glory (esteem, good opinion) deep in God that are given to us by His Spirit as we inquire the living God.
- For example, Enoch searched for God, through faith (seeking unseen practices), until God, through God's unseen practices, rewarded Enoch with translation, to not experience death.

3. The Spirit of God freely gives us the things of God by "perception" (1 Corinthians 2:12).

- In addition, some spiritual understanding is perceived (to know by seeing) from God. The living God will open our eyes to see these things to our benefit.

- For example, Paul healed a man after he perceived the man had faith to be healed (Acts 14:9).

4. The Spirit of God gives us understanding by "spiritual discernment (up-judging)" through "having the mind of Christ" (1 Corinthians 2:13-15).

- One of the ways to understand spiritual discernment (spiritual up-judging) is to understand "down-judging." "Down-judging" is defined or translated as "condemnation" (Romans 8:1). Therefore, "up-judging" discernment can be understood a judging that encourages God's upward (good) opinion of His born-again saints.
- For example, the Church at Thessalonica "up-judged" the teaching the apostles presented through the scriptures (spiritual writings) to make sure what was being taught was correct (Acts 17:11).

HOLY SPIRIT TEACHES

1 Corinthians 2:12-13: *[12]Now we have **not** received the spirit of the world, but the spirit which is '**out-of**' God; that we might know the things that are freely given to us of God. [13]Which things also we speak, not in the words which man's wisdom teaches, but which **the Holy Spirit teaches; comparing spiritual things with spiritual.***

The Holy Spirit teaches with "words" by "comparing spiritual with spiritual." The Holy Spirit teaches us, teaches our spirits, by comparing "things of the Spirit" (spiritual) with other "things of the Spirit" (spiritual). Thus, it is imperative that we define "spiritual" as explained in the Scriptures of Truth.

1. There are "spiritual blessings 'upon-heaven' in Christ" for those "in Christ" (Ephesians 1:3).

- "Blessings" by definition means well-words, good-words, to speak well over someone (our English word "eulogy" is transliterated from this word, except God's heavenly blessings are spoken to us by His Spirit in Christ. An example of these blessings is our "sonship" in Christ, which makes us joint-heirs of God.

35

2. There is spiritual synthesis (comprehensive understanding), as previously discussed (Colossians 1:9).

3. There is God's spiritual house, made of the Living Stone (Jesus) and living stones (believers in Christ); and we offer up to God spiritual sacrifices (1 Peter 2:5).

- God's house is not made up of man-made buildings or some specific location. Teaching that man-made building is God's house is a farce. God's house is made up of people who are "in Christ." Hence, his house is spiritual, made of born-again spirits in Christ in oneness with His Holy Spirit.
- God's spiritual believers also offer up spiritual sacrifices to God (i.e., giving of praises and thanks to God as said in Hebrews 13:15. No more animal sacrifices are required.)

4. The Law is spiritual (Romans 7:14). Man has tried to make the Law of God only[5] a natural function (animal sacrifices). However, the Law is spiritual. For example, the Law of Passover spiritually points to Jesus, our Passover (1 Corinthians 5:7). The Law of Unleavened Bread spiritually speaks to us purging the old leaven of malice and wickedness from our lifestyle. The Feast of Pentecost spiritually speaks of believers in Christ being filled with the Holy Spirit and thus, baptized into the Body

---

[5] There are basically two types of laws of God, redemptive laws, which changes because they point to Jesus Christ and His sacrifices for our sin and sins. There are creative laws that never changes. For example, the creative law of marriage between a man and a woman never changes. Hence, the Laws of God are spiritual (they apply to things of the Spirit of God) as the apostle Paul taught.

of Christ (Acts 2). The Feast of Tabernacles can speak of the resurrection of the saints and also the evangelizing and reaping of nations, bringing them into the Body of God's believers.

5. Gifts of the Spirit are spiritual (Romans 1:11). They help to establish our faith to be mutually on par with apostolic faith to release mutual comfort in us, which is also a spiritual function. In other words, being filled with the gifts and fruits of the Spirit, which is also called "spiritual," comforts us mutually as we minister in these gifts to one another (1 Corinthians 12).

6. According to 1 Corinthians 3:1-3, spiritual is also defined as a person who is purged from the flesh nature of zeal (boiling like a heated pot bubbling), strife (ready to quarrel), divisive (two-standing, two faced, double speech, pitching one preacher against another, denominations, etcetera). Spiritual is also **contrasted against** a neophyte, a babe in spirit. A neophyte spirit is governed by "in part" speech (underdeveloped speech). A neophyte is governed by "in part" disposition (both visceral and cognitive which are not broadened with experience and knowledge). A neophyte spirit is also governed by "in part" logic related to a person's internal reasoning. It follows that a "spiritual" person is broadly developed in the things of God relating to mature speech, mature disposition, and mature logic, which is summed up in one "way," the way of love (1 Corinthians 3:1 w/1 Corinthians 13:9-13).

7. According to the Scriptures (Truth which is written), the rock that the Israelites drank from after Moses smote the rock was Christ. The water, they drank in the wilderness was the spiritual water of Christ. The bread they ate (the Mana)

was spiritual bread, the spiritual bread of Jesus, "spirit words," and the spiritual water of the Holy Spirit (John 7:37-39, 1 Corinthians 10:3-4 w/John 6:53 and John 6:60-63).

SPIRITUAL VS SOULISH

*1 Corinthians 2:14: But the **'soulish'** man **receives not** the things of the Spirit of God: for they are foolishness unto him: neither can he know them, because they are **spiritually discerned**.*

There is a distinction between a soulish[6] believer and a spiritual[7] believer. Or saying it another way, there is a difference between a person who does not have the Holy Spirit, and therefore "soulish," and a person (a believer) who has "the Spirit," and therefore, spiritual. Per the apostle James, a soulish person also exhibits traits of hot bitterness coupled with self-interest.

It follows that the person who is not soulish, because of having "the Spirit of God," can "spiritually discern" (ascertain things by the Spirit of God and by his/her spirit). With that said, we will take a synoptic look at the scripture references that define

---

[6] Soulish (that which is of the soul), per the Lord Jesus, expresses care, worry, sorrow, and so on (Matthew 6); and per the book of James chapter 3, an adverse soul can express hurtful and unpleasant emotions, and so on.

[7] Spiritual (that which is of the Spirit), is related to that which sustains life in the body (James 2), excellent Holy Spirit characteristics (i.e., love, joy, righteousness) (Galatians 5), one's thinking ("the spirit of your mind" (Ephesians 4) good or bad), and so on.

a soulish person and then speak to what it means to "spiritually discern."

Jude 1:16- 19: *[17]But, beloved, remember you the words which were spoken before of the apostles of our Lord Jesus Christ; [18]How that they told you there should be mockers in the last time, who should walk after their own ungodly lusts. [19]These be they who separate themselves,* '**soulish,**' **having not the Spirit.**

Jude stated that there would come a time when some former believers would become grumblers, blaming their fate or lot in life. They will also be considered mockers and walking after their own lusts. With respect to these traits, Jude defined them as **"soulish, having not the Spirit."** That is, the reason why they are considered soulish is that they don't have the Holy Spirit. They are not filled with the Holy Spirit, or they are not baptized with the Spirit, or the Spirit has not yet fallen upon them.

Paul said something similar in Romans 8:9 that the difference between a person "walking in the flesh" (sinful nature) and a person "walking in the Spirit" (divine nature) is "having the Spirit of God." Again, as indicated in a previous chapter, baptism in the Spirit, or the Spirit falling upon us, or being filled with the Spirit, is an utmost imperative. Because when we **"have"** the Spirit in our lives, we are not considered soulish. Also, when we "have" the Spirit, we should pray in the Spirit towards maturing our faith. Jude made this clear when he said in a subsequent verse, "But you, beloved, building up yourselves on your most holy faith, praying **in the Holy 'Spirit'**" (Jude 1:20). Once, we have the Spirit and building our faith in the Spirit, we can then spiritually discern the things of God and receive teachings from the Spirit of God, Himself. With that said, let us briefly look at Apostle James' definition of a soulish person, where James equated the soulish person as also demonically influenced and earthly.

James 3:14-16: *¹⁴But if you have **bitter envying** and **strife in your hearts**, glory not, and lie not against the truth. ¹⁵This wisdom descends not from above, but is earthly, 'soulish,' 'demonic.' ¹⁶For where envying and strife is, there is confusion and every 'foul' work.*

James also defined the soulish person as one who has heated bitterness (or a heated biter, one who is so hot in the **heart** that he/she could bite physically as well as spiritually) and strife (self-interest, debate, and stimulate to anger). These types of soulish traits do not enable spiritual discernment. In fact, the soulish traits disable spirituality (compare 1 Corinthians 3:1-3).

As apostle Paul has also said, "the **'soulish'** man **receives not** the things of the Spirit of God: for they are foolishness unto him: neither can he know them, because they are **spiritually discerned.**" The word "spiritually" in 1 Corinthians 2:14 is an "adverb" (it modifies or describes an adjective). It is only used twice as an adverb, but twenty-six times as an adjective. The only other place besides 1 Corinthians 2:14 where "spiritual" is used as an adverb is Revelation 11:18. Hence, we will use Revelation 11:18 to briefly explain "spiritual discernment."

Discernment is defined as properly, "to distinguish by vigorously **judging "down to up,"** i.e., closely examining (investigating) through "the process of careful study, evaluation and

41

judgment," "to examine, investigate, **question**" (so J. B. Light-foot, Notes, 181f, Biblehub.com). Discernment is translated in some translations as "examined" (as in a court of law), "asking questions," and to "judge."

Thus, per the definition J.B. Lightfoot offered above, one of the processes of receiving and knowing the things of the Spirit is **to ask questions of the Spirit.** We can also examine things thoroughly by **judging "down to up"** with the Lord's spiritual tools (God's Laws, the other scriptures, communing with the Spirit, etc.). We can also receive, know, perceive, and discern the things of the Spirit (spiritual things) by **"comparing spiritual with spiritual"** (1 Corinthians 2:13). We can compare the spiritual scriptures of Truth with other spiritual scriptures of Truth. We can utilize the spiritual gifts to discern the Truth of spiritual activities we may experience. We can attain "spiritual understanding" through the eternal Spiritual One, the Holy Spirit, and so on.

With that said, the only other reference where "spiritually" is used as an adverb, in Revelation Chapter 11:1-14, we learn of the "Two Witnesses" who were eventually killed by the Beast. The Scriptures also said that they were killed in the "great city which **spiritually** is called Sodom and Egypt '**wherever**' also our Lord was crucified" (Revelation 11:8). The use of the words "spiritually" in this verses informs us we must "discern" (up-judge) the verse by comparing spiritual things with spiritual things. It follows that in the Book of Revelation, one entity is called a "great city,"[8] mystery Babylon (Revelation 18:18; 14:8; 16:19).

New Jerusalem is the spiritual "holy city" of the living God, where he also resides. Thus, the "great city" referenced in Revelation 11:8 must refer to mystery Babylon, the apostate harlot system that pretends to be of God (Revelation 17:1-5; 17:18. In addition, this "great city" is also called "Sodom and Egypt." That is, as Sodom, they openly practice sexual perversion like homosexuality, incest, lesbianism; an insensitive lifestyle like abusing the poor; a lazy lifestyle like idleness, and so on (Ezekiel 16:49, Genesis 19). Like Egypt they practice, slavery, killing of godly children (which also selling the souls and bodies of humans), highly developed in sorcery, as Jannes and Jambres, produces satanic deceptions through music (again as Jannes and Jambres), and so on (2 Timothy 3:8, Exodus 7, and Exodus 8).

This means that at the end of the ages (this age included), the "spirituality" of sodomy and Egyptology will be prevalent in the mysterious and religious Babylonian systems of the world. Yet, some of these Babylonians entities will disingenuously claim the voice of the bridegroom (Jesus) and the bride (Jesus' true Church) is in them (Revelation 18:23). However, most of Christ's believers who "have" the Spirit the living God (and therefore they are spiritual) will be able to spiritually discern the unacceptable practices of Sodom and Egypt.

---

[8] Note: Even though the King James translation calls New Jerusalem, a great city, the oldest Greek texts all say, "the holy City New Jerusalem" in lieu of "great city New Jerusalem."

Finally, Revelation 11:8 also said, this "great city" is "where our Lord was crucified." Thus, if one looks at this statement through the lenses of history, this "great city **where** also our Lord was crucified" can **also** point to Jerusalem in the middle east (Jerusalem beneath); and thus, all of the spiritual truth stated above concerning Sodom and Egypt may also apply to some in natural Jerusalem, today (Isaiah 3:9, Isaiah 1:10). Yet, there is also more spiritual understanding to the phrase "**where** also our Lord was crucified." The word "where" (Greek compound: "hopu"—who, which, what (ho) + somewhere (pou)) also means "wherever" and is translated as such in Matthew 8:19, 24:28; 26:13; Luke 9:57, and so on.

Thus, the phase is also rightly translated as "'**wherever**' also our Lord was crucified." This 'up-judging" (examining, asking questions) of all the words the Holy Spirit used in Revelation 11:8 gives a deeper spiritual understanding. Thus, "wherever" our Lord is crucified is "wherever' the peoples of the earth who partake of the sins if the great city, practicing sodomy (i.e., same sexuality, incest) and Egyptian practices [advance sorcery, demonic mesmerizing music, slavery (selling both souls and bodies of humans)] as defined in the Bibie (Genesis 19, Exodus 7, Exodus 8, Isaiah 1, Isaiah 3, Ezekiel 23, Ezekiel 27:13, 2 Timothy 3, Jude 1, Isiah 30, and so on).

SUMMARY OF SPIRITUAL

In closing this brief book on being born of the Spirit. The Lord Jesus taught us that once a believer is born a second time, procreated by the Spirit of the living God, that person is considered as "spirit" (John 3:6). This birthing from above is beginning of "Christ being formed in us" (Galatians 4:19). Therefore we are Christ's when we are born again! Upon being born of the Spirit, as patterned by Jesus, and explained by Paul, John, and Peter (Matthew 1:18, Galatians 4:19, 1 John 5:1, 1 Peter 1:23-25), we must also receive the baptism of the Spirit, just as Jesus also patterned (Luke 3:21-22).

In addition, as it is with natural birth and natural maturation (child, young person, adult), so likewise the born-again spirit of a person also has to mature. This maturity is also produced by the Spirit of the living God with the "spirit" of he/she who is **"just"** [(properly aligning with God's righteous customs) Hebrews 12:23, 1 Thessalonians 5:23].

We also learned that every spirit has a voice, sound, or tone (John 3:8, 1 Timothy 4:1, 1 John 4:1-3). The Holy Spirit has a voice or a sound. Every human spirit has a voice, a sound, or a tone. Every angel spirit (good or evil) also has a voice, sound, or tone. As indicated, the voice of the spirit is different from the voice of the flesh. Yet, the speech of spirit can also be ascertained through a person's speech, spirit scent, spirit cleanness or spirit uncleanness, mildness, or a lack thereof, and so on. There is also spiritual understanding acquired through the Holy Spirit, the Spirit communicating with a believer's spirit (Romans 8:16). God's spiritual understanding can only be acquired through the Holy Spirit and cannot be acquired through the spirit of the world (1 Corinthians 2:11-12). A believer must compare "spiritual with spiritual" to be able to properly discern the things God has for us (1 Corinthians 2:13). And the things God has for them that love him are for "our glory" (our esteem). There is an understanding called "spiritual," "spiritual synthesis" (combining the things of God in a comprehensive logical whole).

Finally, we also briefly discussed "spiritual" versus "soulish," where the soulish person can be defined as a person without the Holy Spirit (Jude 1:19). Jesus made it very clear that when he completed His work and returned to the heavenly Father, it is the Holy Spirit, the Comforter, who would continue the work of the Father and the Son. Therefore, we must allow the Holy Spirit to make His home in us to be considered "spiritual."

*John 16: 7-13: ⁷Nevertheless I tell you the truth; it is expedient for you that I go away: for if I go not away, **the Comforter** will not come unto you; but if I depart, I will send him unto you. ⁸And when he is come, **he will** reprove the world of sin, and of righteousness, and of judgment: ⁹Of sin, because they believe not on me; ¹⁰Of righteousness, **because I go to my Father**, and you see me no more; ¹¹Of judgment, because the prince of this world is judge. ¹²I have yet many things to say unto you, but you cannot bear them now.*

*¹³**However,** when he, **the Spirit of truth,** is come, he will guide you into all truth: for he shall not speak of himself; but whatsoever he shall hear, that shall he speak: and he will show you things to come.*

*John 14:16-18: ¹⁶And I will pray the Father, and he shall give you **another Comforter,** that he may abide with you 'into the age;' ¹⁷Even **the Spirit of truth;** whom the world cannot receive, because it sees him not, neither knows him: but you know him; for he 'remains' with you, and shall be in you. ¹⁸I will not leave you 'orphans:' I will come to you.*

About the Author

Donald Peart is married to Judith Peart. In April 1986, Donald and Judith permanently recommitted their lives to the Lord Jesus. They have been serving the Lord Jesus since and declaring the 'well-message' of Jesus, the Christ. Over the years, the Lord Jesus has worked various manifestations of signs, wonders, and miracles through them.

For a three-and-a-half-year season, the Lord directed Donald to close his small business and to give himself to prayer and study of the Word of God. As a result, Donald, with the strength and insight of the Spirit of Jesus, has studied the Bible for up to eight hours or more per day on a regular basis; and he is still a student of the Lord Jesus.

With that said, the Lord Jesus has also graced Donald to earn diplomas from Baltimore Polytechnic High School; an Associate of Arts degree in Pre-Engineering, a Bachelor of Science degree in Civil Engineering, a Master of Divinity, a Master of Science in Construction Management, and a Doctorate in Theology. Donald and Judith have written over forty (40) books; and they have distributed books in approximately twenty-nine (29) States in the United States, and other nations such as: Jamaica, Italy, Netherlands, Germany, Mexico, Greenland, Tanzania, Uganda, Trinidad, Philippines, India, Peru, Bahamas, United Kingdom, Canada, South Africa, Ghana, Nigeria, Kenya, Australia, France, Sierra Leon, Pakistan, and Brazil.

You can connect with me on:

🌐 https://gibbspublishingconglomerate.com

[f] https://www.facebook.com/drdonaldpeart

Also by Donald Peart

The Bible Old Testament and New Testament Exegete

Readers must be made aware that the italicized words in the (Public Domain) King James Version and within some sections of the King James Version are words that were added by the translators. Another major reason for using the Revised King James Version is that this version points out what has been added or removed by the public domain King James Version. Over the centuries, there are places where proofreaders or publishers missed some of the italics, but for the most part, all added words are italicized. Italicized words were added by the translators in order to convey the complete thought when moving from one language to another.